PIE OF A MOON

Balwinder Singh

This book has been published with all efforts taken to make the material error-free after the consent of the author. However, the author and the publisher do not assume and hereby disclaim any liability to any party for any loss, damage, or disruption caused by errors or omissions, whether such errors or omissions result from negligence, accident, or any other cause.

While every effort has been made to avoid any mistake or omission, this publication is being sold on the condition and understanding that neither the author nor the publishers or printers would be liable in any manner to any person by reason of any mistake or omission in this publication or for any action taken or omitted to be taken or advice rendered or accepted on the basis of this work. For any defect in printing or binding the publishers will be liable only to replace the defective copy by another copy of this work then available.

Illustrations by Kavneet Kaur of Government College of Arts, Chandigarh.

Dedication

Dedicated to the loving memory of my father S. Gurcharan Singh
Bhatia for his silent motivation of reading/listening to good poetry.
He used to enjoy humming couplets of greats like Waris Shah, Bulle
Shah, Ghalib, Shiv Batalvi and

Prof Mohan Singh to name a few.

&

Blessings of my mother Smt Darshan Kaur.

Contents

Preface 9

Acknowledgements 11

1. Pie af A Moon 13
2. All my Childhood 15
3. Absence 17
4. Butterfly 19
5. Change 21
6. Come and Stay 23
7. Cosy Winter 25
8. Darkness 27
9. Days of Life 29
10. Dreams 31
11. Dusk 33
12. Empty Shell 35
13. Footsteps 37
14. Frozen Tears 39
15. Hands that Held Me.. 41
16. Hide and Seek 43
17. Home 45

18. Lantern   47

19. Life in a Bud   49

20. Little Tear   51

21. Making   53

22. Moments of Life   55

23. Night   57

24. Petals   59

25. Praise   61

26. Search   63

27. Silence   65

28. Song of a Life   67

29. Sparkle   69

30. String of Hair   71

31. Sunshine   73

32. The Evening   75

33. The Tree   77

34. Waiting   81

35. Warmth   83

Contents (Hindi)

1. बहुत कुछ — 89
2. चुरा के कुछ हर्फ़ — 91
3. हो जो तू रहनुमा — 95
4. जब भी ये शाम — 97
5. खालीपन — 101
6. खत — 105
7. लफ्ज़ डरते हैं — 109
8. सरद हवा — 113
9. सितारों से आगे — 115
10. रिश्तो का एक और पहलु — 119
11. परिंदो की परवाज़ — 127

Preface

Learned about the beauty of poetry from my father who enjoyed reciting some random couplets of renowned poets in leisure time. With the passage of time, listening to the writings of great poets triggered some thoughts to pen down as a collection.

Right from the greats of all time like Ghalib, Waris Shah, Bulle Shah, Gulzar, Shiv Batalvi to the writers of modern era like Rupy Kaur, Dr Maya C Popa all have brought a refreshing thought to the world of poetry, way of expressing the inner and outer world.

This book is a collection of thoughts that got triggered in my mind while experiencing the influence of great poets in last couple of decades.

Here it is emotions and thoughts cast in words...........

Acknowledgements

To begin my acknowledgements the family comes first having allowed me to use the time in collecting the poetic thoughts and then turning the same into collection. As in my first book "Inkedin Thoughts", my daughter Arpit has edited many of my writings in this book as well.

There has been unconditional support always from wife Sukhwinder and occasional inputs from my son Archit.

Last but not the least big Thanks to my niece Kavneet Kaur "Kina" for drawing the beautiful illustrations for this collection.

Pie af A Moon

Pie of a moon
Moon a fascinating character
of ageless stories
witness of inner monologues
of countless lovers idolised as beloved
an elusive possession within site
but not up for grab
take a pie of a moon
like lover's smile
treasure the sweet and savoury
moments of togetherness
cased in creamy layers of life
as a slice of remembrance.

All my Childhood

All my childhood
and even in adulthood
till I became a father too
could make out
the caged fatherly feelings
lying inside the coconut shell
that also needs a tender touch…

Absence

Since the day
I adopted your absence
it no longer hurts now
your presence in
my remembrance.

Butterfly

The butterfly
hovering around flowers
gave a good chase
before I could make a soft catch
in my fist with trembling nerves
but it slipped away soon
from the fingers
like a beloved in a hurry
leaving behind the impressions
of hurried meeting.

Change

Curse me not
for the changed me
as spread of hopes
with tinge of anxieties
engulfed the teachings
of time and added
layer by layer over me
in becoming myself.

Come and Stay

Come and stay
under my shadow
have spread my arms
to cover your
sun burns
of endless running
for a moment of solitude

Cosy Winter

Cosy winter sunshine
Flowing like a melted
chocolate
Of unspoken words
Fell on white snowy cake
Of silence
Risen up on yeast of
emotions
To make a way through
hearts
For a sweet treat of
remembrance.

Darkness

Darkness knows
that there is a light
resting for the day
on the other side of wall
will wake it up
once I am through with
night
to complement each other's
efforts of keeping
nature's clock

Days of Life

Days of life
Crawling and cuddling
were the days in childhood
squeezed and breathless
become in youthful times
satiated in times of aging
with longer shadows
and unending tales
days now often come and play
as if hurriedness of life
stands tranquilized
open skies and soothing moonlight
whisper symphony in a loving way
'cause days now come and stay.

Image-by Clémence Marollé//Pinterst

Dreams

Dreams engulfed in sweet
memories
travel through the time
taking me to
forgotten lanes as a
traveller looking for
an asylum in someone's
memory

Photo by Sifat Niloy on Unsplash

Dusk

Just before the dusk
when nature was
closing the door on sun
to let the evening
spread its wings
last rays piercing
through door
fell on me
as last act on stage of earth
and then eclipsing everything
me and my shadow.

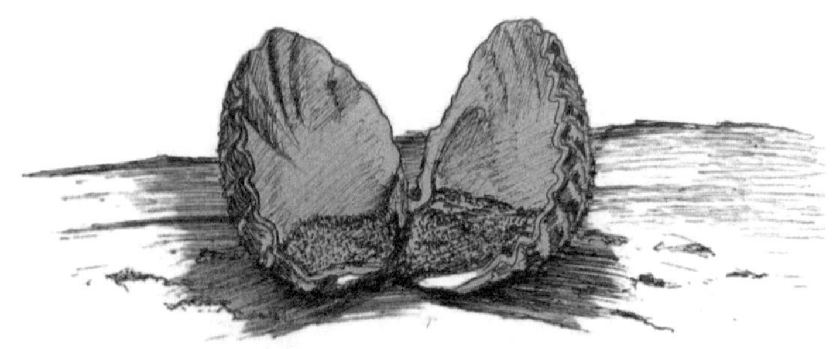

Empty Shell

An empty shell

half-risen day with a timid

sunlight

as someone is pouring his

full- blown breath

in an empty bamboo to dig out some sound

air is moving in the empty shell

but fingers are misplaced to make the sound

eyes still bearing the weight of

unknown dreams

trying to peep out of eyelids

to show being awake

the living in shell as if

nothing exists except thoughts,

nothing is mine that persists

when felt alone in the sea of relations

made friendship with

thyself.................. an empty shell.

Footsteps

Footstep impressions
left on my doormat
on your last visit
haunt the memories
of broken hearts
which could not beat
together.....

Frozen Tears

My fingertips
repeatedly reach out
to corners of eyelids
to push out
the frozen tears
which refuse to go out
as frozen moments
of sweet remembrances.

Hands that Held Me..

Hands that held me

in my unsteady childhood walk

are carrying

all the remembrance in a frail

wrinkled frame….

image by freepik

Hide and Seek

You like a half-risen sun
in long prevailing winters
playing hide and seek
with snow clad memories of
yours
making me to wait
for rays to pierce through
me
and melt myself to turn
into vapour
to rise and meet you up
there.

Home

From womb to the world
housed in different places
nothing stayed permanent
longed for a stay in a place
called home
where I could stay
in memories,
innocent laughter and
a place
of my belongingness

Lantern

Lighting up the lantern
of your memories
went on to find myself
on the lanes travelled together
where did you leave me last?

Life in a Bud

Living life in a bud
was painful wait
so took the risk
of being blossomed
into a flower
and getting plucked
to die in your hands.

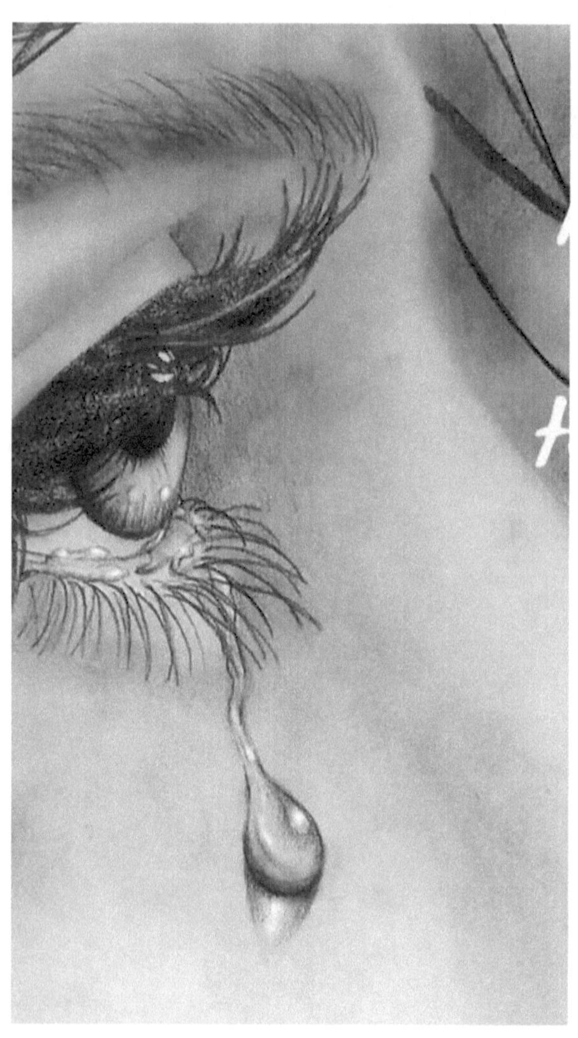

Little Tear

A little tear
struggling with eyes resistance
fell down on cheeks
daring me to hold if I can
but I let it go
to take some pains along
to make way for some more
that may be waiting
in endless wait of yours.

Making

Wet sand assembled
by caring hands
dried in sunshine
of tender love placed with
painters of life
hope, love, hate and anxiety
added shades in canvas
in making of a sculpture
called- a myself of today.

54   ❋   *Pie of a Moon*

Moments of Life

Life is a chain of moments
moments made up of
minutes
minutely carrying seconds of
remembrances that make
moments
some of them fill up the life
and some of them fall
through life
some we admire and keep
while others move out never retreat
ticking of seconds take away years
leave behind the numbers called age
and we remain counting the moments
those stitch through
our life of moments.

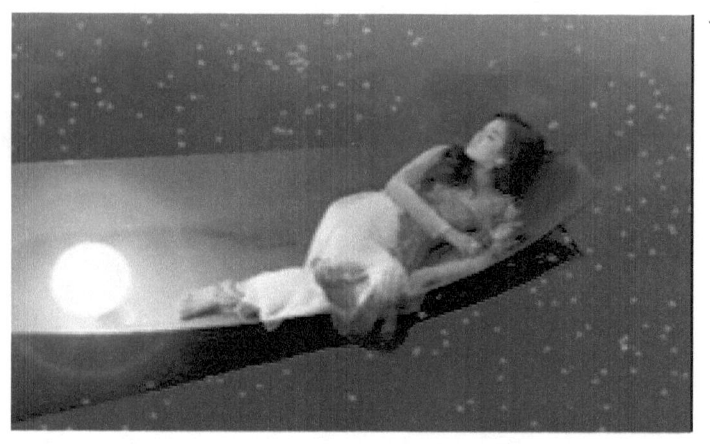

Picture Courtesy-Peakpx.com

Night

Night made a pact
asked me not to bring
sorrows of the day for sleep
and it will always
caress my dreams of
being together.

Image-Shutterstock

Petals

Some petals of words
struck in the rosy lips
lying unspoken like a
broken print of lipstick
left me in
a sea of black silence
forever.

Praise

Praise the pain
praise the labor
praise the sleepless nights
praise the nectar of breast
called milk
praise one of the best creation
of creator
praise thy mother.

Search

Though you were never
missing
from the canvas of my life
but still every colour
became
a pale shadow of your
searching.

Silence

The silence between us
got so loud
that I closed the windows
and door of our house
not to be seen and heard
the way we have agreed to
live through the pause of
our lives.

Song of a Life

Hummed so many times
a new melody in each
rendition
sweet and sour words
added in every interaction
composed by experiences
from rhymes of childhood
and romantics of youth
to full of reminiscences
of silver age.

Image by Harryart on Freepik

Sparkle

The sparkle in your eyes
lightens my way to
go beyond boundaries
and get mixed up in your
heartbeat
as your lips never opened up
to let your heartbeat tell me
"here is your place to stay forever".

String of Hair

A string of hair
from your eyelid
fallen on my hands
I kept it for long
that someday Iwould wish
holding the string in my fist
to exchange the world for
You.

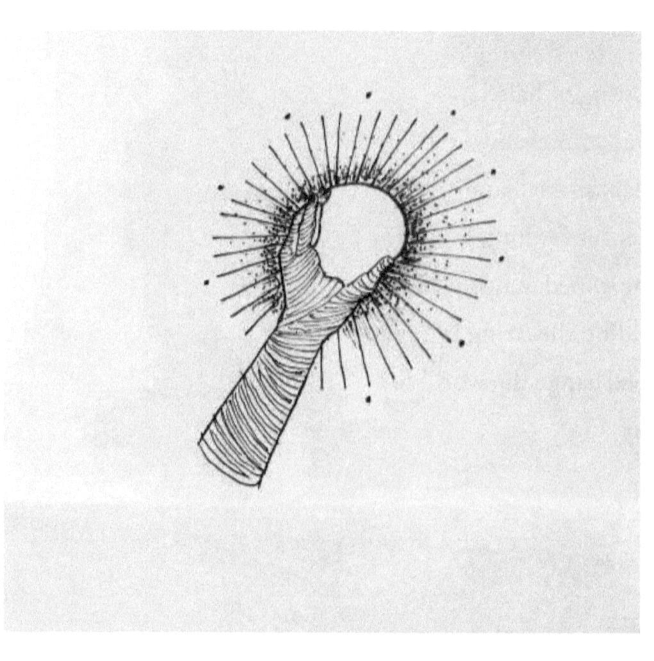

Sunshine

Stolen some sunshine
and put it
in almirah where your
remembrance is kept
to keep your way to home
illuminated
even when darkness
covers my sky.

Image-Wirestock on freepik

The Evening

The evening turned
brown with annoyance
once you left,
started turning dark
for a long night
in empty home turning
everything black
with nothing to be seen
till you come again.

The Tree

Though branches were few

Fruits no more grew

Leaves found tumbling

down

waning strength still held to

ground

like a promise to beloved, to

never depart

blow of wind or a thunder of rain
ailing trunk made a creaky sound
the thought of being left apart
seems to hurt the tree and ground
it stood there in reminiscence of
leaves that now no more grow
and passersby who seek no more shadow
hustling sound of green leaves
all left and tree stood deserted
how many times axe got averted
done its duty as asked by nature
bore the fruits and leaves
and a soothing shadow
for its creatures but roots were
there down and deep
like holding of hands lovers keep

a day will come some axe to wave

its sharpest teeth on my feet

uproot and cut me into logs

to lit up some home or a

deserted street

turn me again into ashes

to meet the companion

again……..the earth

Waiting

The untiring hands of clock
often tells me
not to hate them
as they are my true
companions
in endless waiting for love
as we parted our ways
with a promise
you will keep my love
and I shall keep your
waiting

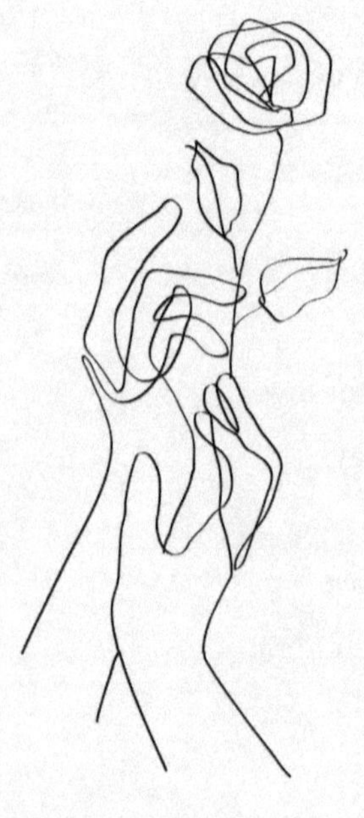

Warmth

The warmth of your
breath
melody of your unspoken
words
caressing touch left in my
hands
is all the treasure
exchanged
for this
life of banishment.

Some wounds refuse to heal
when they carry times gone
by in them…

After snatching even my
share of sky you are saying
i am in the dark….

The rain comes to me
reaching out every pore of
my skin making me a
flowing droplet eager to be
with stream

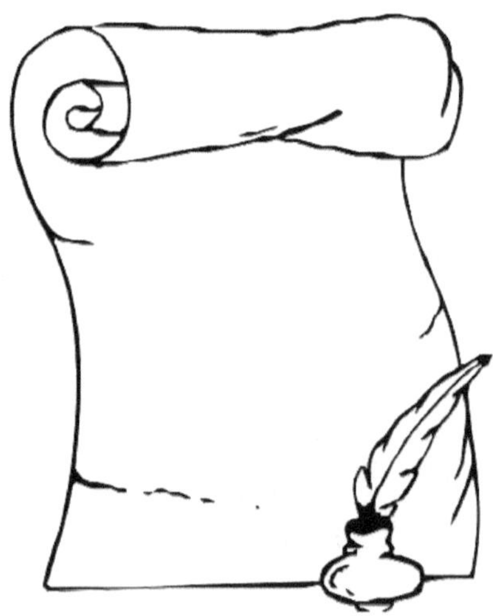

As i fell in love

something rose within me

my gratitude towards human relationships

and nature

for nurturing them.

बहुत कुछ

बहुत कुछ है हासिल मगर
कुछ छूटा सा है
हस्ते हुए चेहरे हैं मगर
दिल खुद से ही रूठा सा है
ढून्ढ रहा है रास्ता
उन छूटे हुए रास्तो में से
जिस गली का निशान मिटा सा है
कई बार उन गलियों में
गुज़र जाता है ये दिल
जैसे मेरे वक़्त का कुछ हिस्सा
वहां छूटा सा है
वो गली वो घर
वो जो सपनो का आशियाँ
कई बार दिल वहां जाने के
सपने बुनता सा है

चुरा के कुछ हर्फ़

चुरा के कुछ हर्फ़ तेरी दिल की किताब से

तेरी गमो की ग़ज़ल कहने दे

मुखढ़ा तो रख लेंगे तेरे जैसा , मुस्कुराता हुआ

अन्तरे में ही सही , मगर दिल की बात कहने दे

कौन सुनेगा यूँ दास्ताँ -ए गम

कुछ अश्यारो में तो मुझे हाल ए -गम कहने दे

बे-पर्दा हुआ जाता है आज कल हर रिश्ता

लफ्ज़ो का ही सही इस पे नक़ाब रहने दे

हो ना सका के चलते चार कदम साथ तेरे

यादों का ही सही मगर साथ , रहने दे

कुछ अश्यारो में तो मुझे हाल ए -गम कहने दे

हर अहसास बयां हो मुश्किल है ऐ दोस्त

नज़्मों में ही सही इन अहसासों को बहने दे

अगर बन जाओ तुम मेरे

हिस्से के आसमान का चाँद

फिर ये ज़माना कुछ भी कहे

.... कहने दे

हो जो तू रहनुमा

हो जो तू हरसफर में रहनुमा मेरा

किश्तियाँ डाल देंगे हम भी तुफानो में

यूँ तो लाखो भरते हैं परवाज़ हर रोज़

कौन बना सका आशियाँ आसमानो में

जो दम भरते थे इश्क़ में फ़ना होने का

कितने बचे हैं इश्क़ के अफ़सानो में

मंज़िलें सर होंगी गर कदम बढ़ाओ

होंसलो की परवाज़ देते रहो अरमानो में

अहसास अपनेपन का और सादगी मोहबत की

ये शह कम मिलने लगी इंसानो में

बदलते रहो तुम भी संग ज़माने के ए दोस्त

पुरानी चीज़े कम बिकती हैं दुकानों में

जब भी ये शाम

जब भी ये शाम यूँ ही ढलती है

गुज़रता दिन हिसाब करता है

दिन तो सिमट के शाम के

आँगन में चला जाएगा

फिर क्यों

लम्हों में जज़्ब होने से मन घबराता है

शाम के आगोश में दिन का यूँ सिम्मट जाना

लम्बे सफर पे निकला मुसाफिर

कुछ पल रुका सा लगता है

ख़तम होने को तो एक वक़्त का कतरा सा है

जो लमह बन के गए वक़्त में सिम्मट जाएगा

बहुत गरूर से निकला था जो दिन बन के

कल के अख़बार के किस्सों में बदल जाएगा

शामे ढल जाती हैं वक़्त का हिस्सा बन कर

यादें जुढ़ जाती हैं

ऐसे उम्र का हिस्सा बन कर

खालीपन

खालीपन है या खुलापन है

कहना मुश्किल है

सपनो का अभाव नहीं

हकीकत की दूरियां है

चलना मुश्किल है

झूठ की बुलंदियों में सच की कमज़ोरिया है

ये बोल पाना मुश्किल है

सपनो की परवाज़ या होंसलो की उड़ान

पंख फैलाना मुश्किल है

विचारो के अच्छे या व्यहोर के सच्चे

इंसान परखना मुश्किल है

मैं अच्छा के मेरी पहचान अच्छी है

इस दुविधा को पार पाना मुश्किल है

चलते रहे हवाएं ले जाती रही जिस और

मुकद्दर के ज़ोर के आगे टिक पाना मुश्किल है

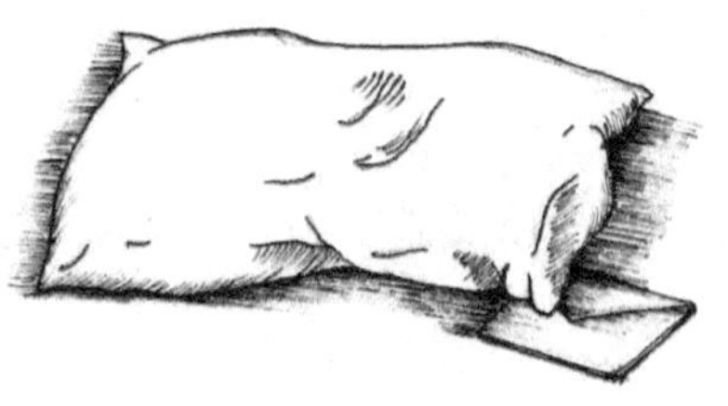

खत

अब तो ना खत है ना खुश्बू है

हर तरफ नुमाइश -ए- मोहब्बत है

इस कदर आसान हो गया है इश्क़

हर पल हर घड़ी अब गुफ़्तगू है

अब कोई अहसास भरे लफ्ज़

कागज़ पे उतारता ही नहीं

अब कोई डाकिआ दरवाज़े पे

नाम पुकारता ही नहीं

कभी छुप के कभी छुपा के

वह खातों को बार बार पढ़ना

कभी रखना किताबो में

कभी तकिये के नीचे रखना

ये लिखावट की मुलाकाते

अब यूँ शायद कोई मिलता ही नहीं

कभी शिकवा कभी शिकायत खत में

कभी पैगाम -ए -मोहब्बत

अब कोई दिल की कलम से

जज़्बात लिखता ही नहीं

जब तुम नहीं होते तो ये खत होते हैं

कई बार तेरी याद में साथ रोते हैं

ऐसे अहसास से अब कोई

भिगोता ही नहीं

बदला ज़माना और बदल गया

ढंग गुफ्तगू का

पल पल बदलता है अब

रंग दिल -ए -आरज़ू का .

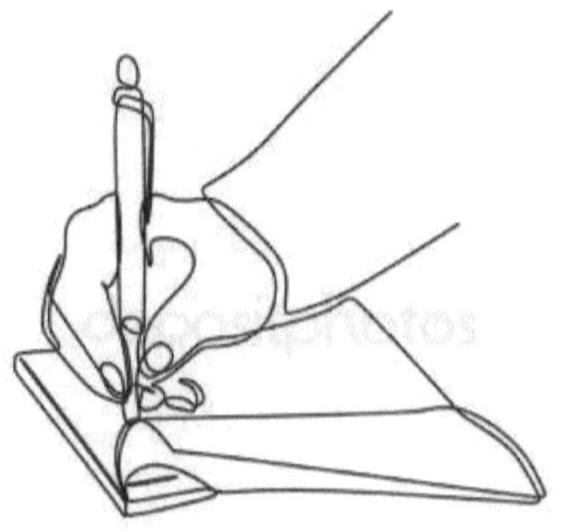

लफ़्ज़ डरते हैं

लफ़्ज़ डरते हैं

ना जाने कितनी देर से सहमे से बैठे हुए हैं

छुप के कलम के अंदर

स्याही की चादर ओढ़ कर

आते हैं कलम के सिरे तक फिर लोट जाते हैं

डरते हैं लफ़्ज़ आजकल कागज़ पे उतरने को

कागज़ कोरा है शायद सफ़ेद झूठ की तरह

लफ्ज़ जो काले नीले है

अजीब लगने लगे हैं सफेदपोशी पे

कौन पूछेगा हैसियत तुम्हारी

इतने बड़े कागज़ पे भला

शोर भारी पढ़ रहा है

चंद लफ़्ज़ों की ख़ामोशी पे

लफ्ज़ जो जनम से ही काले हैं

क्यों उनसे उनके मतलब का रंग पूछते हो

कह लेने दो इनको ज़रा सच

क्यों इन से बोलने का हक़ छीनते हो

रहने दो होंसला लफ्ज़ो के

ज़हन से कलम तक चलने का

कहीं से भी आये रौशनी कायम रहे

सफर लफ्ज़ो के चलने का

लफ्ज़ मिलते हैं कारवां ए ग़ज़ल कहते हैं

मत रोको इनको ये ज़िन्दगी का असल कहते हैं

सरद हवा

सरद हवावों का मौसम है

रिश्तो की गरम जोशी बनाये रखना

दुनिया की आवाज़ों का बहुत शोर है

तुम अपने रिश्ते की ख़ामोशी बनाये रखना

ज़रूरी नहीं हर अहसास बयां हो पाए

बस अपने चेहरे को

दिल का आईना बनाये रखना .

सितारों से आगे

सुनते हैं की सितारों से आगे

जहाँ और भी हैं

इस इश्क़ के इलावा

ज़िन्दगी के इम्तिहान और भी हैं

सिर्फ लफ्ज़ो के हेर फेर से अब

मोहब्बत बहुत देर टिकती नहीं

कमबख्त नेक रूहदारी से भी

हर शै मिलती नहीं

इज़हार करने का होंसला ही

ता उम्र जुटाते रहे

मगर खामोश रह गए

वह जब जब पास आते रहे

वैसे तो वह चेहरे का हर रंग

खूब पढ़ लेते हैं

पर हमारे चेहरे का खत

बिना खोले ही रख देते हैं

आज़माइश तो हर घड़ी

ज़िन्दगी हर पहलु पे लेती है

कभी काँटों से हाथ ज़ख़्मी हैं

कहीं फूलो के हार देती है

कहीं परेशान है ज़िन्दगी

के खामोशियाँ हैं बहुत

कहीं खामोश हो गई ज़िन्दगी

के परेशानिआ हैं बहुत

रिश्तो का एक और पहलु

पेढ़ से ऐसे लगे पतों का टूटना

जैसे किसी अपने से हाथ छूटना

पुराने पत्ते गिर के हवा हो गए

जैसे रिश्ते पुराने खफा हो गए

शाख से लग के हवा से भी डरते ना थे

ज़मीन पे कभी पाँव रखते ना थे

हवाओं संग मस्ती भी खूब की

छू जाती जैसे ज़ुल्फ़ महबूब की

साथ अपनों का बढ़ा प्यारा सा था

पूरा गुलिस्तां बस हमारा सा था

टूट के अलग होना बढ़ा मुश्किल दौर है

हम चल पढ़े जिधर हवाओं का ज़ोर है

पत्तो की तरह ही रिश्ते बिखर जाते हैं

शाख से टूटे हुए पलों में सिमट जाते हैं

छू जाती जैसे ज़ुल्फ़ महबूब की

जो इस तरह से तेरी मोहब्बत का
हासिल होता रहे
फिर ज़िन्दगी से कोई शिकायत
भला कौन करे

----O----

मुश्किल नहीं किसी की
मुस्कराहट का सबब बनना
बस ज़रा सा दिल चाहिए
किसी का दिल रखने के लिए

हर खूबसूरती का हासिल
लाज़िम नहीं
दीदार -ए-चाँद से भी
दुनिया का गुज़र होता है

----O----

वह कुछ इस तरह से
ज़िन्दगी समझने लगा है
की ज़िन्दगी भी अब पूछती है
के कौन सा दर्द बाकी है

सब के हिस्से में आसमान बराबर का है
मिलेगा उसको जिसके होंसलो में उड़ान होगी

----O----

एक आज़ादी ऐसी भी
हाँ तुम आज़ाद हो
कुछ भी कहने को
मगर जुबान खुले तो
बस मुझ से पूछ कर

चिराग जला के इंतज़ार रात भर का था

दिल जला के इंतज़ार उम्र भर किआ

----O----

एक क़तरा पी लिया

जो उस नज़र से

कम्भख्त ज़माना ता उम्र

शराबी समझता रहा

परिंदो की परवाज़

आजकल आकाश में परिंदो की

परवाज़ कम हो गई है

लगता है फ़िज़ा खुशगवार नहीं है

कुछ चहकना भी अब कम

सुनाई देने लगा है

जैसे घोंसलों के बाहर अब

आसमान नहीं है

हस के बोलने का मतलब

कुछ और तो नहीं

परिंदो को भी हम पे

ऐतबार नहीं है

मिलने जुलने की फितरत

शायद छूट रही है

कैसे कह दे परिंदो से के

हम कसूरवार नहीं हैं

कुछ पल मिल के बैठे

तो हक़ जताने लगे

इंसानो की तरह परिंदे भी

रिश्तो से आज़ाद नहीं हैं